a

Practical Guide

to

Dockers

---

by

Shiv Kumar Goyal

Preface

Welcome to the world of Docker containers. This book is designed to be your comprehensive guide to understanding Docker containers, their usage, deployment, and best practices.

In recent years, Docker has revolutionized the way software is developed, shipped, and deployed. With its lightweight and portable containerization technology, Docker has become the go-to solution for building, packaging, and distributing applications across different environments seamlessly.

Whether you are a developer, system administrator, or IT professional, this book will provide you with the knowledge and skills necessary to harness the power of Docker containers effectively. From the fundamentals of containerization to advanced topics, each chapter is carefully crafted to provide you with practical insights and hands-on examples.

Key topics covered in this book include:

1. Understanding containerization and Docker fundamentals
2. Building Docker images and managing containers
3. Docker networking and storage
4. Continuous integration and delivery with Docker
5. Monitoring and troubleshooting Docker environments

How to Use This Book

This book is structured to take you on a journey from the basics of Docker containers to advanced topics, with each chapter building upon the previous ones. Whether you are a beginner looking to get started with Docker or an experienced user seeking to deepen your understanding, you will find valuable insights and practical examples throughout the book.

Each chapter begins with an overview of the topic and its importance in the context of Docker containers. This is followed by step-by-step tutorials and hands-on exercises to help you apply what you've learned in real-world scenarios.

Who Should Read This Book

This book is suitable for anyone interested in learning about Docker containers, regardless of their level of expertise. Whether you are a developer, system administrator, DevOps engineer, or IT manager, you will find valuable insights and practical guidance to enhance your skills and advance your career.

Conventions Used in This Book

Throughout this book, we use certain conventions to help you navigate and understand the content more easily:

Command-line examples: Commands you can run in your terminal are formatted like this: `docker run -d nginx`.

File paths and code snippets: File paths and code snippets are formatted like this: `~/myproject/docker-compose.yml`.

Syntax: Syntax of commands are formatted like this:
- `docker pull [OPTIONS] NAME[:TAG]`

Feedback

Your feedback is invaluable to us as we strive to improve this book and provide you with the best possible learning experience. If you have any questions, comments, or suggestions, please don't hesitate to contact us at **1skgoyal@gmail.com**.

We hope you find this book informative and enjoyable. Let's dive into the exciting world of Docker containers together!

Happy containerizing!

Shiv Kumar Goyal

Contents

Introduction 1

System requirement 10

Docker Desktop 12

Docker Engine 17

Important Concepts.. 22

Important commands 25

Managing docker Images... 33

Building images 38

Docker Networking 46

Docker Volume 50

Debugging a container 57

Docker Compose 61

Container registries 67

Deploy our containerized app 75

Chapter 1

Introduction

An operating system is a piece of software that controls your computer's hardware resources. An operating system is a layer that sits between applications and hardware. Any application requires an operating system on your computer to function. Microsoft Windows, Apple Mac OS, Unix, and Linux are some of the operating systems available on the market. Traditionally, we install any of the aforementioned operating systems on compatible hardware. On top of this operating system, we load the desired program, together with its dependencies and configuration files. However, Docker has revolutionized the way applications are deployed in the echo system.

What exactly is Docker?
Docker is an open-source virtualization program that uses containers to simplify application development and deployment. To accomplish this, the application is packaged in a container with all of its dependencies, settings, tools, and runtime, allowing for easy sharing and deployment. The term "container" refers to a sandboxed process that is isolated from all other processes running on the host machine. Process isolation is achieved by using the Linux namespaces and cgroups capabilities. Containers run natively under Linux and share the host computer's kernel with other containers. It

relies on the host kernel, which is why it is lightweight, and it shares resources with other containers, allowing for better use of hardware resources.

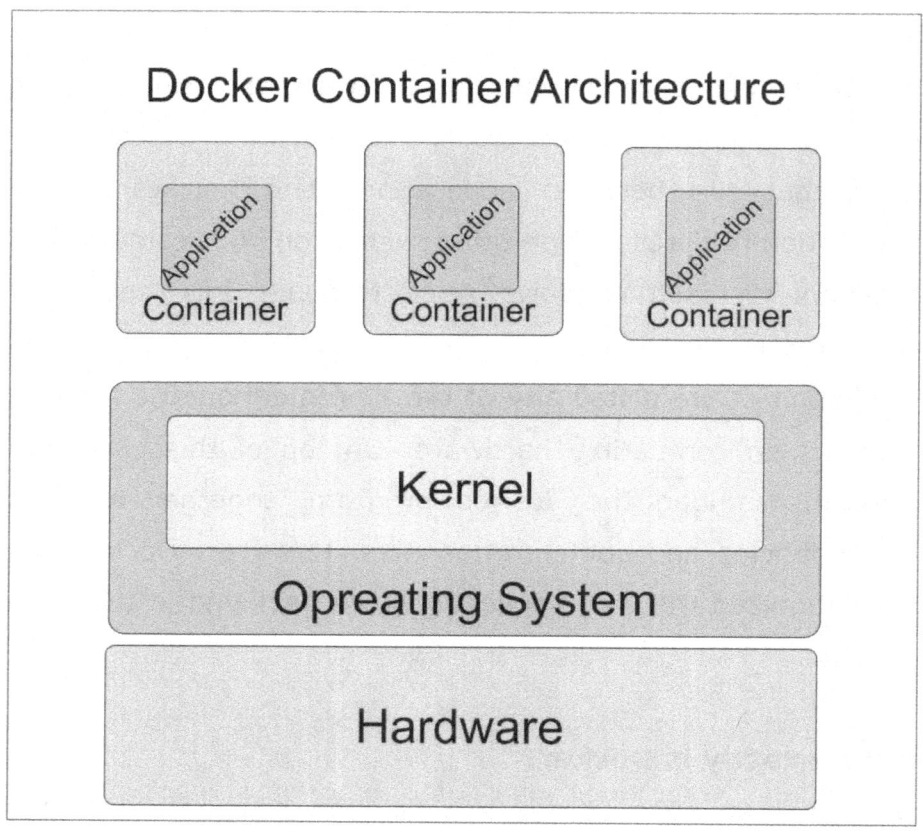

Why Docker?

Containers simplify the process of updating and upgrading the application. It is not just an upgrade in case of any issue; it also simplifies the rollback process.

To develop an application without using a Docker container, a developer must first install and setup all services on the operating system itself. Assume a developer is working on a

Java program that requires a database and Java software; he must first install all of these services on his or her local workstation or development server. When he moves the same program from development to testing and finally to production, he must install all components in both environments. In practice, delivering all of these components spanning diverse work contexts is a tough and time-consuming task. This procedure consists of numerous steps, each of which has the potential for failure. Furthermore, providing the same version of libraries and configuration files across multiple environments presents an enormous challenge.

Docker solves the dependency problem by encapsulating all essential libraries and configuration files in a container. As a result, each container runs in a separate environment from the other containers. You can run multiple containers on the same machine for redundancy purposes; if one instance fails, the next available instance can be used.

Benefits of Containers
- Containerization
- Portability
- Consistent results across platforms
- Better efficiency
- Isolation
- Reduced IT management
- Microservices Architecture
- DevOps Practices

- Improved application development
- Vibrant ecosystem and a large community of users

Overall, Docker has revolutionized the way software is developed, shipped, and deployed by providing a standardized, efficient, and portable platform for building and running applications in containers. Its benefits in terms of portability, efficiency, isolation, and ecosystem support make it a popular choice for modern software development and deployment workflows.

Comparison between container and Virtual machine

Virtual machines (VMs) and other virtualization technologies can sometimes be confused with container technology. Containers and container technology are not the same, despite some basic similarities.

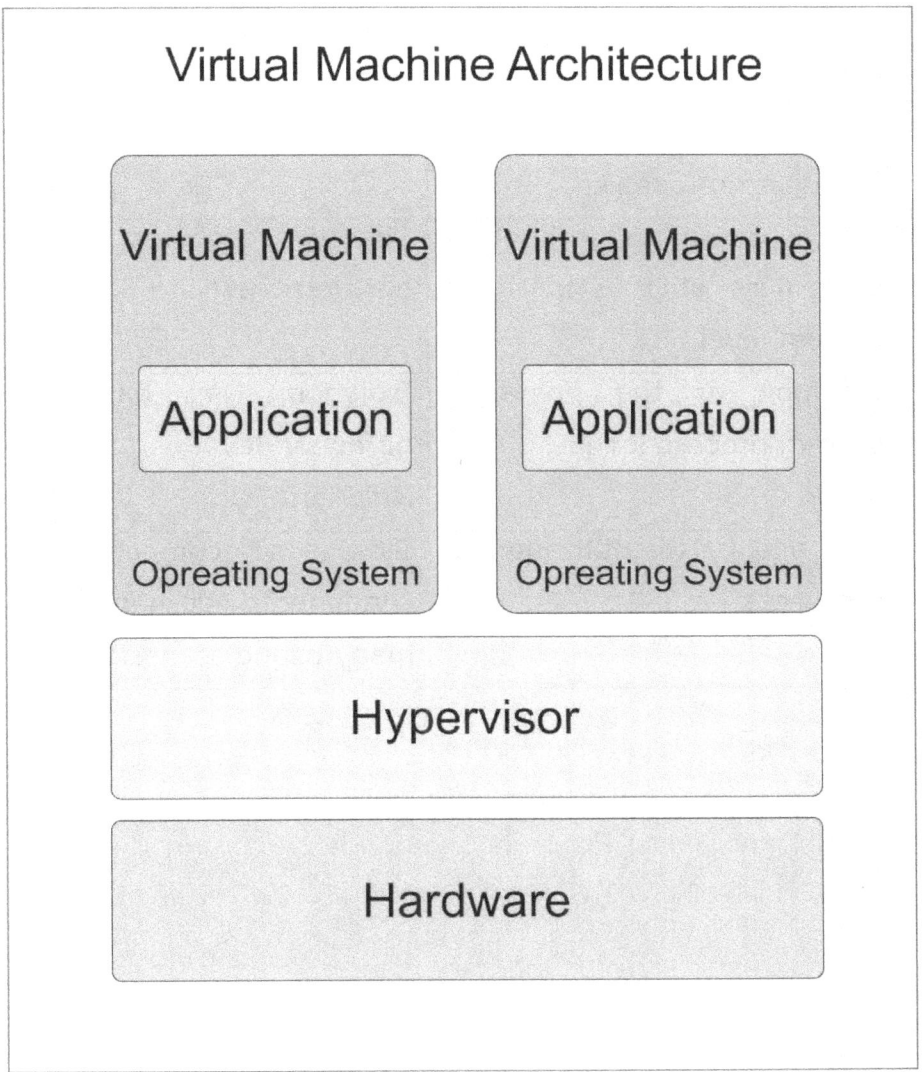

The differences between virtual machines and containers are as follows:-

Container	Virtual Machine
It relies on the host kernel.	Runs on a hypervisor with its own operating system.
Contains an application along with all of its dependencies (binaries, libraries, configuration, etc.).	A virtual machine contains an entire operating system.
Shares resources with other containers at the operating system level.	Shares resources at the hardware level.
Isolation at the operating system process level.	Isolation is based on hardware-level process isolation.
Fast and better utilization of resources.	Slow in comparison to containers, yet necessary in many usage scenarios.

Docker Architecture

Docker is built on a client-server architecture. The Docker client and server communicate using the REST API. The server manages and runs the containers. The server and client can run on the same system or on different workstations.

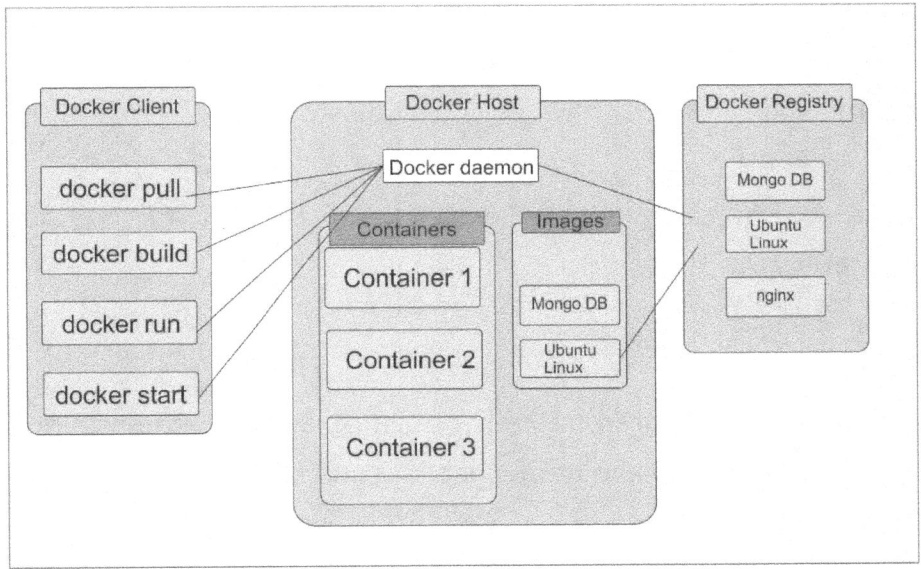

The Docker Engine consists of two main components:

Docker Daemon (dockerd): The Docker server includes a Docker daemon (dockerd) that listens to client requests both locally and across the network. This background service runs on the host machine and manages container-related tasks such as container lifecycle management, image handling, networking, and storage.

Docker CLI (docker): The Docker command-line interface (CLI) is used by users to interact with the Docker Daemon. It allows users to build, run, and manage Docker containers using simple commands.

While Docker was originally designed to run natively on Linux, it's important to note that Docker has expanded its support to other operating systems as well. Docker provides native support for Windows and macOS through Docker Desktop, allowing users on these platforms to run Docker containers seamlessly.

Here's a quick overview of Docker's support for various operating systems.

Linux:

Docker containers run natively on Linux, as Docker uses Linux kernel capabilities like namespaces, control groups (cgroups), and union file systems (e.g., OverlayFS) to support containerization.

Windows:

Docker Desktop for Windows supports running Windows containers natively on Windows Server and Windows 10 (Pro, Enterprise, and Education editions).

Windows containers use kernel characteristics native to Windows, such as Windows Server Containers (process and namespace separation) and Hyper-V Containers (lightweight virtualization).

macOS

Docker Desktop for Mac supports running Linux containers natively on macOS. Docker Desktop for Mac uses a lightweight Linux virtual machine (based on Alpine Linux) running in the background to host Linux containers, enabling developers.

Other Operating systems

Docker also supports other operating systems that use various virtualization technologies, such as VMware and VirtualBox. The virtualization technologies allow users to run Docker inside a virtual machine running Windows or any supported Linux distribution.

Chapter 2

System requirement

The system requirements for installing Docker vary depending on the operating system. However, for optimal machine performance, you should have more resources than this.

For Windows
- Windows 10 64 bit Pro, Home or Education edition 21H2 (build 19044) or higher.
- Windows 11 64-bit: Home, Pro, Enterprise or Education version 21H2 or higher.
- WSL version 1.1.3.0 or later.
- At least 4GB RAM optimally 8GB of RAM or higher
- 64-bit processor with Second Level Address Translation (SLAT)
- 50 GB of free Disk Space.
- BIOS-level hardware virtualization support must be enabled in the BIOS settings.

For mac
- macOS must be version 11 or higher
- 4GB RAM
- VirtualBox version 4.3.30 or later

For Linux

- A 64-bit installation of one of the following versions of Ubuntu: 20.04 LTS, 22.04, 23.04, 23.10
- A 64-bit installation of Debian 9 or newer
- A 64-bit installation of CentOS 7 or newer
- 4GB or more RAM
- 30GB free disk space

Docker Desktop

Docker Desktop is an easy-to-install program for Mac, Linux, and Windows environments. It has a simple graphical user interface (GUI) that allows you to manage your containers and images directly from your machine. In addition to the GUI mode, Docker Desktop also supports the Command Line Interface (CLI). Docker Desktop enables simple installation and configuration on your desktop PC, allowing you to focus on application development rather than spending time installing and configuring your development environment. Although Docker Desktop is a free software, commercial use of Docker Desktop at a company with more than 250 workers or more than $10 million in annual revenue requires a paid membership.

Benefits of Docker desktop
- Simple and quick installation.
- Integrated Development Environment (IDE):
- The ability to distribute applications across many cloud platforms.
- **Local Development and Testing**: Docker Desktop enables developers to build, run, and test containerized applications locally on their machines.
- **Cross-Platform Compatibility:** Docker Desktop enables container portability between platforms,

allowing for smooth integration with various development environments
- Volume Sharing and File System Integration
- **Orchestration**: Docker Desktop integrates with container orchestration tools such as Docker Compose and Kubernetes, enabling users to define, deploy, and manage multi-container applications and Kubernetes clusters locally. This container orchestration support facilitates the development and testing of complex, distributed applications in a controlled environment, improving scalability, reliability, and performance.

Installation Process

We will discuss how to install Docker on a Windows 10 computer in this chapter. Docker Desktop installation is a pretty easy and straightforward process. The following is a summary of the steps required to complete the installation:

1. Install wsl

    To install WSL, first open the command prompt and type the following command:-

    ```
    wsl --install
    ```

2. Download the Docker Desktop installation file from the below link.

https://www.docker.com/products/docker-desktop/
3. Double click the downloaded file.
4. On the prompt, select WSL instead of HyperV.

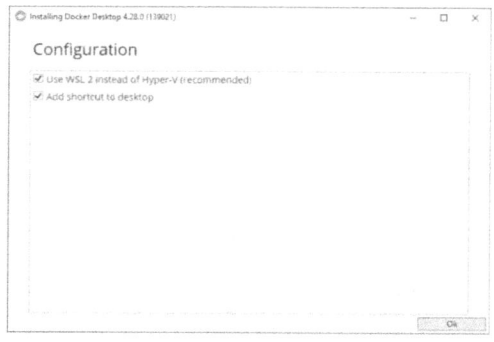

5. Follow the installation wizard and press **Close** on completion of the installation process.

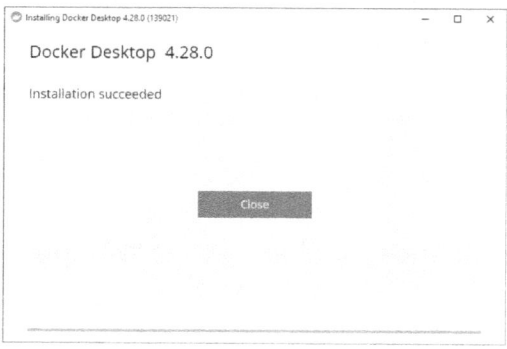

6. If your current user does not have administrator's rights, then switch the Docker-user account to an administrator account. In settings, select Local Users and Groups > Groups > Docker-users.

7. Launch the Docker desktop by clicking the Docker desktop icon. Select "Use recommended settings" and click the Finish button.

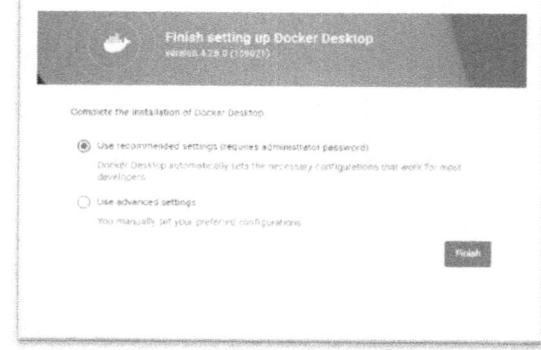

8. Once it is started it will show screen like bellow:

If you get an error updating the WSL, give the following command at the command prompt

`wsl --update`

To verify the installation

At the command prompt

`docker run hello-world`

If this command runs successfully, then your installation is doing well.

The newly created container will be visible in the Docker desktop interface.

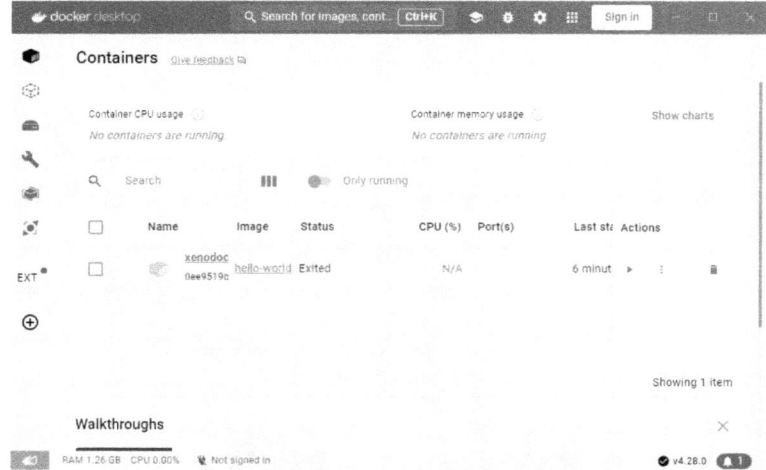

Chapter 4

Docker Engine

Docker Engine is an open-source containerization platform that can be used to develop and containerize applications.

Core components of Docker

Docker Engine is a client-server program that includes three main components:

- A server running the dockerd daemon process.
- The Docker Engine REST API allows applications to interact with the Docker daemon. It can be accessed with an HTTP client.
- A command line interface (CLI) Docker client.

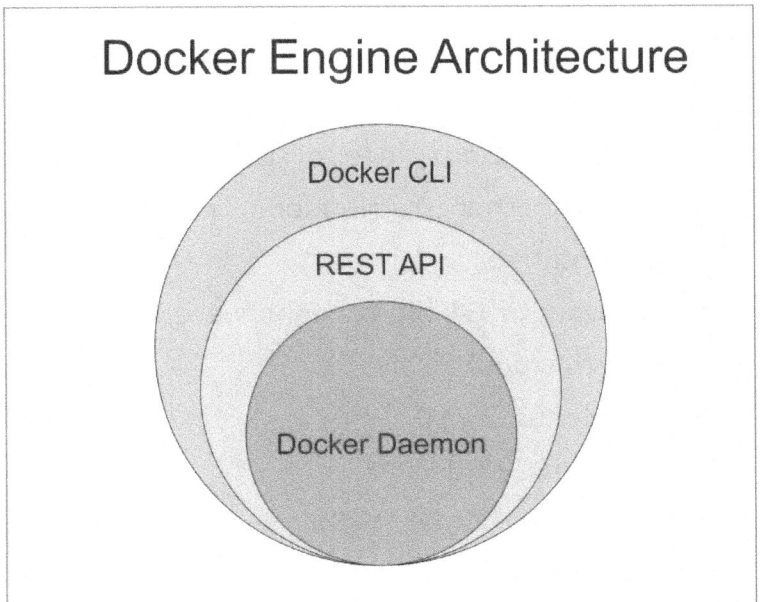

Difference between Docker desktop and Docker Engine.

Docker Desktop, as the name suggests, is for desktops, or you can say it is for use in development and test environments. Docker Desktop provides a GUI interface and is used on the desktop PC of the developer or tester. Whereas the Docker engine is for servers where you want to load your application as microservices for production.

Docker Engine on Linux

The Docker Engine supports the following Linux distributions:
- Centos
- Debian and some of its derivatives, like Linux Mint.
- Fedora
- Ubuntu and some of its derivatives.

In this section, we will discuss the Docker engine installation process on Ubuntu Linux, one of the most popular Linux distributions. For other distributions, please refer to the Docker documentation.

The following Ubuntu 64-bit versions were supported at the time of writing this book :-
- Ubuntu Mantic 23.10
- Ubuntu Lunar 23.04
- Ubuntu Jammy 22.04 (LTS)
- Ubuntu Focal 20.04 (LTS)

If the system already has an old version or unofficial incompatible packages installed, uninstall them. A list of packages that must be removed before installation follows:-
- docker.io
- docker-compose
- docker-doc
- podman-docker
- containerd.io
- runc

Command to uninstall the above packages
```
$ sudo apt remove docker.io docker-compose docker-doc podman-dockercontainerd.io runc
```

Remove the storage directories if they are already there.
```
$ sudo rm -rf /var/lib/docker
$ sudo rm -rf /var/lib/containerd
```

There are two ways to install Dockers on Ubuntu:
- Install using the convenience script.
- Install from a package

Install using the convenience script

Install curl command if it is not already there.
```
$ sudo apt install curl
```

Go to the Downloads directory of the current user.
```
$ cd ~/Downloads
```

Make a temp directory in the Downloads folder and change it to the temp directory.
```
$ mkdir temp
$ cd temp
```

Download the script in the current directory
```
$ curl https://get.docker.com -o get-docker.sh
```

Now run the script. You require an administrator's account password to run this command.
```
$ sudo sh get-docker.sh
```

Manage Docker as non admin user

This is an optional step if you wish to run the Docker command without using the sudo prefix. You may add the current user to the Docker group.
```
$ sudo usermod -aG docker $USER
```

To verify if the current user is part of the docker group
```
$ sudo cat /etc/group |grep docker
```

After this command, you have to logout and login again to get the effect of the above command, or you can use the following command to re-evaluate the current user.

```
$ newgrp docker
```

Verify the installation

```
$ docker run hello-world
```

If you receive, a permission denied error due to the sudo command used during installation, run the following command to troubleshoot the issue:

```
$ sudo chown "$USER":"$USER" /home/"$USER"/.docker -R
$ sudo chmod g+rwx "$HOME/.docker" -R
```

Configure the Docker daemon to start at boot automatically.

```
$ sudo systemctl enable docker.service
$ sudo systemctl enable containerd.service
```

Check the status of the Docker daemon.

```
$ sudo systemctl status docker.service
$ sudo systemctl status containerd.service
```

Chapter 5

Important Concepts

Before we dive deeper into Docker, let's go over a few important concepts that will help you understand it.
- Docker image
- Docker registries
- Docker hub
- Container

Images

Images are read-only templates containing instructions for creating a container. The Docker image includes both the operating system and applications. The image is comparable to a virtual machine template, which represents a stopped virtual machine. The Docker build command is used to generate images. Layers may be present in Docker images above the base image. You can store images on the Docker registry.

Difference between image version and tag

A Docker tag assigns a unique identifier to a Docker image. A Docker repository contains collections of similar images with varying versions, which are distinguished by tags. Tag is a unique, human-readable manifest identifier for a specific version or variant of an image.

Multiple tags

A single image can contain many tags. Typically, the latest tag provides the most recent version of the image. For example, the Ubuntu version 22.04 image has 22.04, jammy-20240111, jammy, and latest tags pointing to the same location.

Container

The running instance of an image is known as a container. You use the Docker run command to start a container. It provides the environment to run the application. It contains all the binaries and dependencies we need to run our application.

Container vs Image

Most of us use these terms interchangeably, yet there is a small difference between the two.

A container is an image's running environment. To launch an application, we typically need binaries, configuration files, a file system to save log files, and temporary files, as well as environmental configuration and variables. So the container provides all of the necessary items. Containers also require port binding to communicate with the environment outside the container. The container has its own operating system with a virtual filesystem that is segregated from the host OS. Here It is important to mention that the host is the system running the container. Generally, images have more than one layer. As previously said, each image has its own version and tags.

Docker registries

Registry is a centralized storage solution for images. You can host your own private registry or use Docker's public registry (Docker Hub). It can contain Docker images with the same name but different tags; each tag denotes a version of the image; for example, nginx contains tags 1.25.3, mainline, 1, 1.25, latest, and so on.

Docker Hub (Registry)

The Docker Hub is an official public repository for Docker images. Docker Hub is a service provided by Docker for finding and sharing container images. It gives clear and necessary documentation for the stored images. Docker Incorporation has a dedicated staff that reviews image contents. It also provides security updates in a timely manner.

These are some of the key concepts; we will be exploring more concepts in depth later in this book.

Chapter 6

Important commands

In this chapter, we will look at some of the most common commands used in Docker operations. We will look at the following common operations to manage Dockers using the Docker command line:
- Download Image
- Create container
- Start container
- Stop Container
- List images
- List containers
- Access a running container
- Remove container
- Rename container
- Accessing container
- View logs of container
- Getting help and information

Downloading an image

As previously stated, images are stored in a central repository, either public or private, and must be downloaded before running. If the image is not already present locally, you can download it using the Docker client's **docker** command. Go to the command prompt and type the **docker pull** command with the image and tag names. The tag name is optional; if you do

not specify one, the latest image will be downloaded by default.
Syntax:

```
docker pull [OPTIONS] NAME[:TAG]
```

Options:
–all-tags, -a: It downloads all images with different tags in that repository.
-help : to get help about the command

Example
```
$ docker pull ubuntu:jammy
```

To create and run a new container from an image, we use the **docker run** command. The beauty of this command is that it can also download the image if it is not already there.

There are many options for the run command. By adding attributes to the run command, you can configure it to run in detached mode, change its name, mount a volume, and perform a variety of other actions.
Syntax
```
docker run [OPTIONS] IMAGE [COMMAND] [ARG...]
```

-d, -detach: This option runs the container in the background and prints its ID.
-h, -hostname: is used to alter the container's hostname.

-e, -env: sets the container's environment variables.

-i, -interactive: It allows you to interact with the container.

-l, -label: This adds metadata to the container.

-name: It specifies the container's name.

-mount: This option is used to mount a filesystem to the container.

Example

```
docker run nginx
```

other example

```
docker run -name nginx-production nginx
```

To stop the container, press Ctrl+C in the command prompt or terminal window

List the running containers

Once container is running you use the **docker ps** command displays a list of all currently running Docker containers. You can also use "docker container" ls as an equivalent command to achieve the same results.

Syntax

```
docker ps [options]
```

Options

Short	Option	Description
-a	--all	The option displays all containers, including stopped ones, whereas the default without -a only displays those that are currently running.

-n	--last	Shows n last created containers
-l	--latest	Shows the latest container

Example
```
docker ps
```

As previously stated, the "docker ps" command displays all running containers; however, if you want to view the list of both running and stopped containers, use the -a option.

```
docker ps -a
```

The above command displays a list of all containers, including their ID, image name, and status.

Start a container

The "docker start" command can be used to start one or more stopped containers. You can also use the "docker container start" command to achieve similar outcomes.

Syntax
```
docker start [options] container_id/ container_name
```

Example
```
docker start ubuntu1
```

Stop a container

To stop a running Docker container, use the docker stop command, followed by the container name or id.

Syntax
```
docker stop [OPTIONS] Container_id / Container name
```

Example
```
docker stop ubuntu1
```

This command will gracefully stop the container and free up all resources utilized by it.

Remove a container.

To remove a stopped container that is no longer needed, run the "docker rm" or "docker container rm" command.

Syntax
```
docker rm [options] container name/ ID
```

Options

Short	Option	Description
-f	--force	Forcefully remove the running container.
-v	--volumes	Remove volumes associated with a specific container.
-l	--latest	Shows the latest container.

Example
```
docker rm ubuntu1
```

This will permanently remove the container and its associated resources.

Renaming Existing Containers

When you run a container with the docker run command without name option, Docker automatically assigns a random name. Use docker rename to change the name of a running or stopped container from a random or undesirable name to something meaningful. This command allows you to give the container a new name while keeping its configuration and data.

Syntax

```
docker rename Container_name new_name
```

Example

```
docker rename magical_sanderson nginx-production
```

Access a running container

To access an already-running container and execute a new command, use the docker exec command. There are many options that you can use with this command.

Syntax

```
docker exec [options] container_id/ Container_name command
```

Options

Short	Option	Description
-d	--detach	Run command in the background
-e	--env	Set the environment variables.
-i	--interactive	Shows the latest container.
-t	--tty	Allocate a pseudo TTY
-u	--user	Give command as different user
-w	--workdir	Working directory inside the container

Example
```
docker exec -it ubuntu1 bash
```

The above command launches a bash shell within the container, allowing us to execute commands and navigate the container's file system.

```
docker exec -u user1 ubuntu1 whoami
```

This command will run whoami as the user1 user within the container.

View container logs

The docker logs command allows you to inspect the logs generated by a Docker container. When a container starts, it begins writing log messages to its STDOUT and STDERR streams. The command's output displays logs with data from the output stream along with a timestamp.

Syntax
```
docker logs [options] container_name/ container_ID
```

Options

Short	Option	Description
-f	--follow	Shows the logs in real time.
	--since	Show logs since timestamp.
-n	--tail	displays the number of lines from the log's end.

Example

```
docker logs -f 8f64d692b852
```

Getting help and information

To get help about any command, you can use the --help or -h option with any docker command.

docker [command] --help

Example

```
docker images --help
```

Display system-wide information about docker installed on your system. The information includes the number of containers, images, and docker versions installed.

```
docker info
```

Chapter 7

Managing docker Images

Docker images are read-only templates with instructions for constructing a container. A docker image is an immutable snapshot of the file system. The Docker image consists of a temporary filesystem and its own private network address. It has its own process group that operates within the containers. Each image has its own randomly generated unique hex ID. Images can be labeled with human-friendly names. Each image can be assigned multiple tags.

Images management commands
In this section we will dive in to some of the crucial commands for docker image management.

List all locally available images
Get a list of all locally available images.
`docker images`

You can also use different syntaxes to list images
```
docker image list
docker image ls
docker images
```

Example
To filter the Docker images by tag
`docker images ubuntu:latest`

Search images at Docker hub

Docker Hub is Docker's public repository for storing Docker images. http://hub.docker.com allows you to search for and read detailed information about any image.

You can also use the docker command-line tool to search the Docker Hub for an image.

Syntax
```
docker search [options] <image name>
```

Example
```
docker search ubuntu
```

You can filter the output using –f or --filter option.
```
docker search -f stars=5 ubuntu
```

View image history

As images contains multiple layers stacked on top of each other. Each layer represents a specific change to the file system inside the container such as creating a new file or altering an old one. Once a layer is created, it becomes immutable, which means it cannot be altered. To list the image history and show all it layers:-

Syntax
```
docker history image_name
```

```
docker history nginx
```

View detailed information

Use the "docker inspect" command to access low-level information such as configuration and runtime details about Docker objects (containers, images, volumes, networks, etc.).

Syntax

```
docker inspect container_name/container_id
```

Example

docker inspect b690f5f0a2d5

Tagging an image

As mentioned, you can give human readable tags to an image

Syntax

```
docker tag image_name tag
```

Example

docker tag ubuntu1 20.03

You can also create image from a container using bellow command.

Syntax

```
docker commit container image
```

Example

docker commit ubuntu1 ubuntu2

Delete the Image

To remove an image that is no more required you can use "docker image rm" command. You can also use following equivalent syntaxes to remove image.

```
docker image remove
docker rmi
```

Syntax

```
docker image rm image_name
```

Example

```
docker image rm ubuntu1:latest
```

Remove all unused images

To delete unused and dangling images that are not referenced by any container, use the "docker image prune" command.

Syntax

docker images prune [options]

Options

Short	Option	Description
-a	--all	Remove all unused images, not just dangling ones. Use this option with caution.
-f	--force	Do not prompt for confirmation

Example

```
docker image prune -a
```

A docker image name consists of two parts: "REPOSITORY:TAG". The TAG section specifies the image's version. If not specified, the default is ":latest".

Transferring images

Images for Docker are kept in a repository. Using repositories, you can distribute container images to the public, your client, and other team members.

Use the pull command to transfer an image from the repository to your local host.

Syntax

```
docker pull [OPTIONS] NAME[:TAG]
```

Options:

–all-tags, -a: It downloads all images with different tags in that repository.

-help : to get help about the command

Example

```
$ docker pull ubuntu:jammy
```

Using the push command and the image's name or tag, transfer the image from the local host to the repository.

Syntax

```
docker push repository-user/repositoy-name:tag
```

Chapter 8

Building images

Docker builder relies on BuildKit, which is part of Docker Engine. The builder is used for creating container image or other artifacts. The builder uses context as input. The context provides all of the information needed to handle resources on the daemon.

At the client level, the "docker build" command generates a Docker image from a Dockerfile using docker daemon. A Dockerfile is a text file that contains instructions for Docker to build an image. This command also sends to the Docker daemon any additional files and directories that are present in the current directory.

Syntax

`docker build [options] PATH`

The PATH argument determines the location of the Dockerfile and build context.

Options

Short	Option	Description
-f	--file	Path to the Dockerfile to use.
-t	--tag	Specify name (and optionally with tag) for target image.
	--pull	Pull the latest base image

Example
```
docker build -t ubuntu/nginx:1.19 .
```

In the above example, ubuntu is the repository name, nginx is the image name, and 1.19 is the tag. The dot(.) at the end of the command specifies that the Dockerfile is located in the current directory. If the Dockerfile is located in a different directory, specify the path instead.

```
docker build -t nginx:1.19 .
```

In this example, we are only using the image name and tag.

DockerFile

A Dockerfile is a text file containing a collection of instructions that Docker utilizes to create a Docker image. The Dockerfile specifies the base image to be used, the files to be copied into the image, additional packages to be installed, environment variables, ports settings, and commands, among other things. To add arguments, use the # symbol at the start of the line.

Creating a Dockerfile

You will need a simple text editor to generate a text-based file with no file extension that contains a script of instructions. The steps involved in this script are shown below:-
- Select a base image .
- Set the working directory.
- Install the packages required for your application.
- Copy the application files.

- Set the environment variables.
- Expose the necessary ports.
- Provide the command.
- Specify entrypoint.

Select base image

In this step you select the existing base image to be used. Other option is to create your own.

Set the working directory

The WORKDIR instruction specifies the directory used by the subsequent commands, such as RUN, CMD, ENTRYPOINT, COPY, and so on. You can have multiple WORKDIR instructions in a Dockerfile. WORKDIR can be either absolute or relative.
Example

Install the packages required for your application

The RUN instruction is used to install all of your application's dependencies, including additional packages installed through package managers such as apt, yum, or pip. It adds a new layer on top of the current image, which is utilized in the next instructions.
Example
```
RUN apt install -y curl
```

Copy the application files

The COPY statement copies files or directories to the image. This instruction is commonly used to copy application code and supporting files to an image. This statement consists of two parameters: source and destination.

`copy myapp /mydir/`

To modify the ownership and permissions of destination files, use the --chown and --chmod arguments when copying myapp to /mydir/.

Example

`COPY --chown=myuser:mygroup --chmod=644 myapp /mydir/`

Set the environment variables

The ENV instruction sets the environment variable. If your program requires any environmental variables to be set, you can use the ENV instruction to accomplish this. You can use multiple ENV statements in a Dockerfile to set multiple environment variables.

Syntax

`ENV <key>=<value>`

Example

`ENV MYNAME="Shiv Kumar"`
`ENV XDG_SES="C2"`

Expose the necessary ports

The EXPOSE instructions in the Dockerfile specifies the network port on which your application will listen at runtime. By default, the EXPOSE instruction assumes a TCP port, but you can specify UDP ports.

Syntax
```
EXPOSE port [port/protocol]
```

Example
EXPOSE 8080/TCP
EXPOSE 8080/udp

You can override the defined ports at runtime by specifying the -p option in the docker run command.

Example
docker run -p 8081:8081 ubuntu1

Provide the command

The CMD instruction allows you to specify the command to be executed when executing a container from an image. The Dockerfile should only contain one RUN instruction; if you specify multiple RUN instructions, the last one will take effect.

Syntax
```
CMD command param1 param2
```

Example
CMD ["echo", "Hello"]

Specify entrypoint

The ENTRYPOINT instruction, like CMD, specifies the command to be performed when the container is launched. However, ENTRYPOINT does not allow you to modify the command, whereas CMD may be overridden by inserting your own parameters to the docker run command.

Example

```
ENTRYPOINT ["echo", "Hello"]
```

Example of Dockerfile

```
# Select the base image
FROM ubuntu:latest

# Set the working directory to /project
WORKDIR /project

# Install dependencies for your application
RUN apt-get update
RUN apt-get -y upgrade
RUN apt install -y apache2
RUN apt install -y apache2-utils
RUN apt clean

# Copy the content of current directory
COPY . /var/www/html

# Expose the ports
EXPOSE 80

# Set the Enviroment
ENV APACHE_LOG_DIR /var/log/apache2

# Use CMD to start the apache
CMD ["apache2ctl", "-D", "FOREGROUND"]
```

Building a docker image from a Dockerfile

Use the docker build command in the same directory where the Dockerfile is located to build an image from a Dockerfile.

Steps for building an image

1. Create a Dockerfile for your application, as explained earlier.
2. For ease of access, move the program files to the current folder. Another option is to specify the location of the application files in the Dockerfile.
3. Run the docker build command in the same folder where dockerfile is located.

Syntax

```
docker build -t <image_name>
```

Example

```
docker build -t ubuntu-apache .
```

4. Wait for the build image process to finish.
5. Verify the newly created image with the docker images command.

Syntax

```
docker images
```

Example

```
$ docker images
REPOSITORY        TAG       IMAGE ID        CREATED            SIZE
ubuntu-apache     latest    79307ee59e95    50 minutes ago     241MB
```

6. **Start the container**

    Once the image is complete, you can launch the container to validate it.

```
docker run -d -p 80:80 ubuntu-apache
```

7. Check the container

In this example, we copied customized index.html to the /var/www/html folder. To check if the site is working, open a web browser and navigate to localhost. You should now see your customized website page.

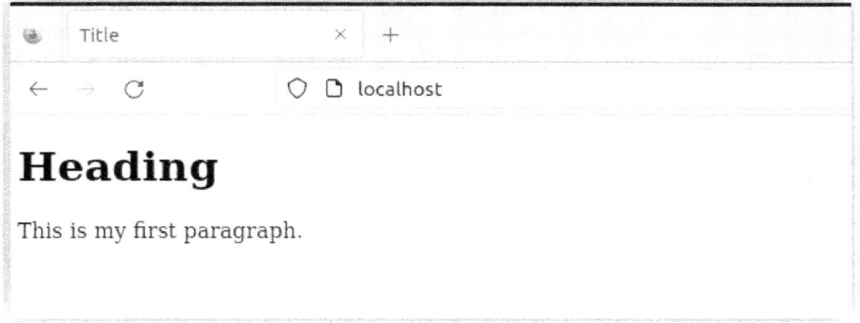

Chapter 9

Docker Networking

Docker networking enables you connect containers to one another and to the outside world. Docker networking allows you to create a variety of network types, which facilitates a wide range of typical use cases. Below are some common Docker network types also known as network drivers:

Network Type	Description
bridge	This is the default network, which facilitates communication between containers and the private network with the host.
host	Creates a network between the host and the container, which shares the host's network stack (namespace).
none	Completely isolate the container by disabling all networking
overlay	Useful in connecting multiple Docker hosts.
ipvlan	The IPvlan driver provides users with full control over both IPv4 and IPv6 addressing.
macvlan	Assign MAC address to a container. Usefull in many user cases where mac address is required on physical network.

User defined network and container network

Custom network allows you to isolate different groups of containers. Container networks can be used for inter-container communication in addition to user-defined networking methods. Use the --network container:<name|id> option with the docker run command. You can use the docker network command for managing docker networking.

To list all existing docker networks on your host, use the following command:

`docker network ls`

Use the docker network create command to create a custom network. This command requires a unique network name.

Syntax

```
docker network create network_name
```

Example

`docker network create app_net1`

You can also create networks for specific drivers with specified subnet masks.

`docker network create -d bridge --subnet 10.0.0.0/24 net-bridge`

Once network has been created you can verify the newly created network using docker network ls and docker inspect commands.

`docker network ls`
`docker inspect net-bridge`

To connect a container to newly created user defined network use --network option with run command.

Syntax

```
docker run --network=network_name image_name
```

Example

docker run -dt --network=net-bridge --name c1 ubuntu-apache

Create another container from same image on same network

docker run -dt --network=net-bridge --name c2 ubuntu-apache

Check the IP address of the newly created container.

Syntax

```
docker inspect container_name /ID
```

Example

docker inspect c1

This command will show low-level information containing the IP address and other details.

To show only the IP address of the container.

Syntax

```
docker inspect   -f '{{range.NetworkSettings.Networks}}{{.IPAddress}}{{end}}' container
```

Example

The example below shows the IP addresses of the containers.

```
docker inspect   -f '{{range.NetworkSettings.Networks}}{{.IPAddress}}{{end}}' c1
docker inspect   -f '{{range.NetworkSettings.Networks}}{{.IPAddress}}{{end}}' c2
```

Connecting Docker to an outside host

In many circumstances, you need to connect the container from outside the host, or the container has to communicate with other containers across the hosts; in this scenario, the host network driver is useful.

To create host network use --network=host option

Syntax
```
docker run -dt --network=host --name container_name image
```

Example
```
docker run -dt --network=host --name c3 ubuntu-apache
```

You can now access the application running on the container from outside the host using the host IP address and the port exposed by the application.

Chapter 10

Docker Volume

Every Docker image contains layers of read-only filesystems. Each layer represents the difference in the layer below it. Layers are stacked on top of each other to form the basis for a container's root filesystem. Docker stores image layers via storage drivers and provides a single, unified view. When generating a new container from the image, a thin, writable image is built on top of the Docker image's layer stack. This thin layer is used to write files into the container, including log files and packages. However, deleting the container also deletes the readable layer, leaving the underlying images intact. If you want to keep your data persistent (intact), there are two ways to do it:
- Bind mount
- Volumes

Bind Mount

In the case of a bind mount, we specify a path to both the host and container virtual file systems. Bind mounts let you store data anywhere on the host. In contrast to volumes, a non-Docker process can alter the data. Bind mounts cannot be managed directly using the Docker CLI. Bind mounts can be quite beneficial in the following scenarios:-
- Sharing configuration files
- Sharing source code

- Where fie and directory structure consistency is required.

Syntax

```
docker run -dt \
--mount type=bind, src=host_PATH directory, target=Mount_point \
--name container \
Image
```

Example

```
docker run -dt --mount type=bind,\
src=/home/volume/data, target=/vol1 \
--name c1 ubuntu-apache
```

Volumes

The most effective method to keep data persistent is to employ volume. These volumes can be used to store persistent data, such as databases and other stateful data. If we use volume, the data persists even after we remove the container. To put it simply, volumes are mounted directory paths on the virtual filesystem of the container. As a result, any data saved on the container's mounted path is automatically saved in the host directory. The advantage of employing volume versus maintaining data on a thin layer is the easy movement of data from one container to another, or even to other hosts. Volume drivers enable you to store volumes on distant systems or cloud providers. Volume drivers also enable encryption of volumes' contents.

Types of volumes

Anonymous volume

Anonymous volumes are created without specifying a container path or name; the host path is established automatically by the dockers. A directory is automatically generated in `/var/lib/docker/volumes/random_hash/_data`.

Anonymous volumes are frequently used to store temporary or transient data generated by containers throughout their lifecycle.

Named volumes

Named volumes are created and managed using a user-specified name and source (host path). Named volumes allow containers to share data autonomously. In the production environment, it is typically advised to use named volumes.

In addition to these, there are more types of Docker volumes:

Remote Volumes

Remote volumes are created and handled on a remote host. This facilitates data exchange between various Docker hosts.

Third-Party Volume Plugin

Third-party volume plugins allow you to store docker volumes on external storage systems such as cloud storage or distributed file systems.

Manage volumes

Create volume

To create a volume, use the create option of the "docker volume" command.

Syntax

```
docker volume create volume_name
```

Example

docker volume create volume1

Once the disk has been created, you can verify it with the ls command option.

Example

docker volume ls

To get low level information about the volume

Syntax

```
docker inspect volume_name
```

Example

docker inspect volume1

Remove the volume that is no longer necessary.

Syntax

```
docker volume rm volume_name
```

Example

docker volume rm volume1

Start a container with a volume

To start the container with volume, use either the --mount or -v options.

The -v option consists of three fields separated by colon characters (:), which must be in the correct order.
- The first field is the volume name for named volumes and optional for anonymous volumes.
- The second field indicates the path or directory on the host that has been mounted.
- In the third field, select the option to read and access the mounted volume.

Example

```
docker run -dt -v volume1:/vol1  --name c1 ubuntu-apache
```

--mount option require multiple key-value pairs separated by commas. The options are
- type

    Type of mount that can be bind, volume, or tmpfs
- source
- destination
- readonly

Example

```
docker run -dt \
--mount source=volume1, destination=/vol1 \
--name c1 \
ubuntu-apache
```

In some case volume has to mounted read only to protect the data consistency. To mount the volume read only

```
docker run -dt \
--mount source=volume1, destination=/vol1, readonly \
--name c1 \
ubuntu-apache
```

The examples above are of named volumes; however, if the need arises for an anonymous volume, you can omit the source.

Example

```
docker run -dt -v :/vol1   --name c1 ubuntu-apache
```

Bind mount

```
docker run -dt -v /home/volume/data:/vol1   --name c1 ubuntu-apache
```

Examples to demonstrate volume

Create container and volume
```
$ docker run -dt -v volume1:/vol1 -name c1 ubuntu-http
```

Connect to container
```
$ docker exec -it c1 bash
```

Change the directory
```
# cd vol1
```

Create a file
```
# touch c1iop
```

Logout from the container
```
# exit
```

List the volumes
```
$ docker volume ls
DRIVER      VOLUME NAME
local       volume1
```

Stop the container
```
$ docker stop c1
```

Remove the container
```
$ docker rm   c1
```

Check the volumes to see if the volume is still exiting.
```
$ docker volume ls
DRIVER      VOLUME NAME
local       volume1
```

Create new container with same volume
```
$ docker run -dt -v volume1:/vol1 --name c2 ubuntu-http
```

Connect to the new container and navigate to the folder
```
$ docker exec -it c2 bash
# cd /vol1
# ls -la
total 8
drwxr-xr-x 2 root root 4096 Mar 11 06:00 .
drwxr-xr-x 1 root root 4096 Mar 11 06:04 ..
-rw-r--r-- 1 root root    0 Mar 11 06:00 c1iop
```

```
# exit
```

Chapter 11

Debugging a container

So far, we've seen how containers may help developers quickly construct and run cross-platform applications; yet, running error-free programs on containers remains a persistent problem. If you're new to Dockers, debugging them may seem daunting. In this chapter, we will illustrate how to tackle many of these troublesome issues and obtain the superpower of mending containers.

Using the CLI

You can inspect the container in interactive mode to detect any issues. You may also utilize intrusive sessions to debug and gather system information. If you want to know the container's IP configuration and other network parameters, use the -it option with the run command, or if the container is already running, use the exec command with the -it option.

Syntax

```
docker exec -it container_id bash
```

or

```
docker exec -it container_id /bin/sh
```

This will provide you with a command shell from which you may execute any Linux command. If the command is not already installed, you can install it.

Example
```
docker exec -it ubunt1 bash
```

Docker attach

The docker attach command is another way to connect to an already running Docker. The Docker attach command launches a terminal session while the container (and any programs it contains) is running.

Syntax
```
docker attach container_id/ container name
```

Example
```
docker attach 7896807d8084
```

The difference between the exec and attach commands is that the attach command only starts one session, while the exec command allows you to create multiple shell sessions.

Monitoring resource usage

When an application is operating slowly or misbehaving, checking the system resources is the best place to start. The Docker stat command is identical to the classic Linux top command for containers.

Syntax
```
docker stats
```

If you want to check the resource usage of a specific container, you can add a container ID or container name with docker stats command.

Example

`docker stats 7896807d8084`

Monitoring processes in a container

You can use the top command to inspect the details of all running processes in a container, similar to the ps function in Linux.

Syntax

`docker top container_ID / Container_name`

Example

`docker top 7896807d8084`

To view the formatted output, add faux.

`docker top 7896807d8084 faux`

To get the list of processes running as any specific user.

`docker top container_id -u username`

Example

`docker 7896807d8084 -u root`

View the logs

Linux logs provide a visual history of everything that has occurred within an operating system and its running programs. So, if something goes wrong, logs provide a useful overview of events that can assist you in identifying the problem or monitoring the system. To inspect the logs of the container, the docker logs command is available.

Syntax

```
docker logs container
```

Example

docker logs 7896807d8084

The command above will display the logs that were present at the time of execution.

To examine continuous logs and track new entries arriving in logs.

Syntax

```
docker logs --follow container
```

Example

docker logs --follow --tail 10 7896807d8084

The above command examines the container logs and displays the last ten lines. To exit this command, hit the Ctrl + C keys.

Chapter 12

Docker Compose

In general, an application is composed of multiple components. A single web application, for example, could include a http server, a database server, and extra service servers. Managing an application in a container environment with multiple containers running to meet application requirements is a tremendous task. Furthermore, each container must be manually started and connected together for inter-container communication. To address these issues, Docker offers Docker Compose, a framework for defining and running multi-container applications that allows you to manage services, networks, and volumes in a single, understandable YAML configuration file, simplifying control over your entire application stack. You can start and create all of the services from your configuration file with a single command.

Docker compose allows you to manage the entire life cycle of your application.
- Building and rebuilding services.
- Start and stop services.
- Monitor service status and handle logs.

How compose works

Docker compose uses YAML or YML files. In the present version, this file is named compose.yaml or compose.yml; in prior versions, it was known as docker-compose.yaml or docker-compose.yml. The default path for a Compose file is in your working directory.

Install Docker compose

There are two ways to install Docker Compose:-
- Install Docker Desktop.
- Install the Compose plugin.

Install docker desktop

If you are using docker desktop, docker compose is already installed, thus there is no need to do anything.

Install the Compose plugin

If you're using the Docker engine, you can either install the Compose plugin from the Docker repository or manually download docker-plugin.

Install using docker repository

For Ubuntu and Debian

`sudo apt install docker-compose-plugin`

For RPM-based distros like Red hat Linux , run:

`sudo yum install docker-compose-plugin`

To download manually

If you need to download a binary file directly, use the curl command.

```
curl -L \
"https://github.com/docker/compose/releases/download/v2.24.6/docker-compose-linux-$(uname -s)-$(uname -m)" \
-o /home/shiv/docker-compose
```

Here, the download directory, /home/shiv/, can be changed to any directory where you want to save the downloaded binary files.

Next, we need to provide the downloaded Docker Compose file execute permissions. Go to the download directory and run the following command:

`chmod +x docker-compose`

Once installed, you may verify the version.

`docker compose version`

Creating Your First Docker-Compose File

Now let's create our first Docker Compose file. You can build one with your favorite text editor, such as Vim. To generate the compose file, execute the following command:

`vim compose.yaml`

Add the following content to the file.

Example 1

```
version: '3'
services:
hello_world:
image: ubuntu
command: [/bin/echo, 'Hello world']
```

In the above example, the hello_world service is initialized from the ubuntu:latest image and just runs echo 'Hello world'.

Example 2

The example file below installs two container services, Redis and PostgreSQL, using two networks: backend and frontend.

```yaml
version: "3"
services:

  redis:
    image: redis:alpine
    ports:
      - "6379"
    networks:
      - frontend
    deploy:
      replicas: 2
      update_config:
        parallelism: 2
        delay: 10s
      restart_policy:
        condition: on-failure

  db:
    image: postgres:9.4
    volumes:
      - db-data:/var/lib/postgresql/data
    networks:
      - backend
    deploy:
      placement:
        constraints: [node.role == manager]
networks:
  frontend:
  backend:
```

Identifier	Description
version	Specifies the version of the compose.yaml file. Several variants of the compose file format are known, including 1, 2, 2.x, and 3.x.
services	The Services section identifies required services..
app	The app section specifies a custom container name..
image	The image that needs to be pulled.
Container_name	Container_name refers to the name of each container.
restart	Starts/restarts a service container.
port	Port specifies the custom port for running the container.
working_dir	The current working directory for the service container.
environment	Defines environment variables to configure application settings and other parameters such as database credentials, etc.
command	The command to run the service.

Build and run your application with Docker Compose.

```
docker compose up -d
```

This command initiates the container creation process by referring to the docker-compose.yml file in your local directory.

Using the `docker ps` command, you can verify that the containers are up and running.

You can test your application once it is up and running.

To stop the services, use the following command

```
docker compose stop
```

Container registries

A Docker registry is a system that stores and distributes Docker images under specific names. The Docker Registry solves the long-standing challenge of managing and organizing container registries. The Docker registry can contain many versions of the same image, each with their own set of tags. A Docker registry is organized into Docker repositories, each of which contains every modification of a given image.

The Docker registry is used to acquire images locally, and you can submit your own images to the repository if you have the necessary rights. The pshed images can be distributed both internally and publicly. The Docker registry is generally classified into two types: private and public. Private repositories have restricted user access, whereas public repositories are accessible to anybody. By default, the Docker engine connects to Docker Hub. Docker Hub is Docker's public cloud registry service, where you may find Docker images created by other communities.

The registry is a server-side application for storing and distributing Docker images. It is stateless and highly scalable.

Apart from Docker, numerous organizations provide paid online Docker registries for public use. These organizations are typically cloud providers with registries as one of their services. Some other Docker registries are:-
- Amazon Elastic Container Registry (ECR)
- Google Container Registry (GCR)
- Azure Container Registry (ACR)

Using the Docker repository to publish custom images.

In this part, we will walk you through the process of using the dokcer repository to publish your custom images to Docker Hub.

Create an account on the docker hub at the following website. https://www.docker.com/pricing?utm_source=docker&utm_medium=webreferral&utm_campaign=docs_driven_upgrade

Create a repository for keeping your images.

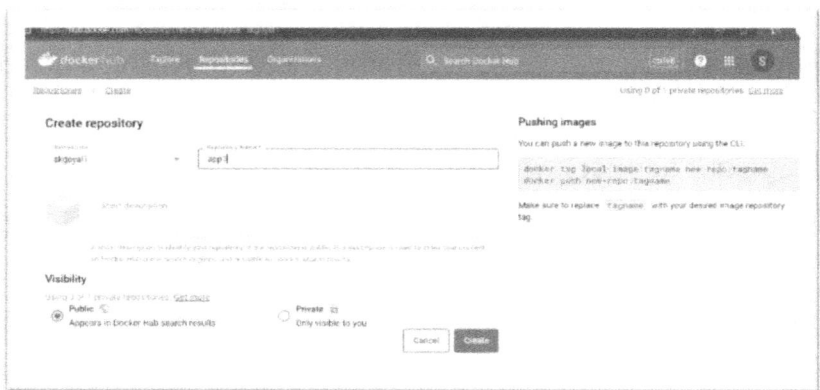

Login in to docker account

```
$ docker login
```

```
Log in with your Docker ID or email address to push and pull
images from Docker Hub. If you don't have a Docker ID, head
```

```
Username: skgoyal1
Password:
```

Tag images on your local system with the username and repository of Docker Hub.

```
$ docker image tag nodejs skgoyal1/app1:nodejs
$ docker image tag mongo-express skgoyal1/app1:mongo-express
$ docker image tag mongodb skgoyal1/app1:mongo
```

Push the image to docker repository

```
$ docker push skgoyal1/app1:nodejs
$ docker push skgoyal1/app1:mongo-express
$ docker push skgoyal1/app1:mongo
```

As these images are now published on the cloud, they can be used anywhere, such as in a production or testing environment.

Log into your Docker account on the server where you wish to use the image.

Create a compose file or manually launch the container in the new environment.

```
$ docker run --name express  skgoyal1/app1:mongo-express
```

To use third party registry

Previously, we used Docker Hub as a registry; in this section, we will learn how to use a third-party private registry for containers. We'll utilize Amazon ECR as an example. To use Amazon ECR, you must have a basic familiarity with the AWS console. The method below demonstrates how to push (upload) an image to ECR for other team members to use.

- Login to the AWS console.
- Create an IAM policy with permissions (List, Read, Write) for the Elastic Container Registry.
- Create an IAM user.
- Create Group.
- Add newly created policy permissions to this group.
- Add this user to the newly created group.
- Get the access key and secret key for this user. Keep these keys safe.
- Install AWS CLI on your local Docker host machine.
    - Download the awscli zip file

```
curl "https://awscli.amazonaws.com/awscli-exe-linux-x86_64.zip" -o "awscliv2.zip"
```

    - Unzip the downloaded file

```
unzip awscliv2.zip
```

    - Run the downloaded file to install AWS CLI

```
sudo ./aws/install
```

- Confirm the installation with the following command.

```
aws --version
```

- Run the aws configure command and provide the access key, secret key, region, and JSON as responses on the prompt.
- Check if the terminal is connected to your account.

```
aws configure list
```

- Go to the AWS console and search for the Elastic container registry.
- Under Create repository, click Get Started.

- Leave everything as default and just provide the repository name. In this example, we will provide the repository name as ubuntu-http and click **Create repository**.

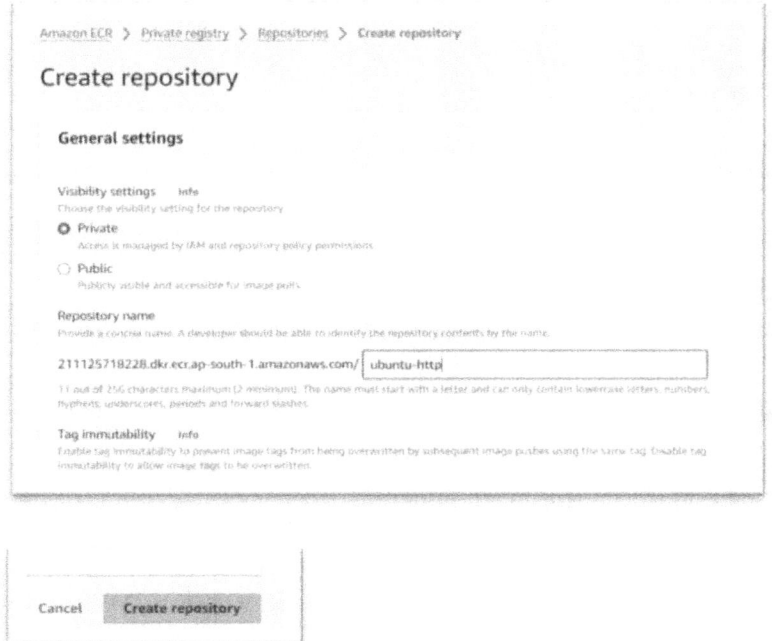

- Choose the newly created repository and click View Push Commands.

Copy the first command and paste it on the CLI; this will connect the Docker client to the repository. (This command should be given in a single line.)

Syntax

```
aws ecr get-login-password --region region | docker login --username AWS --password-stdin aws_account_id.dkr.ecr.region.amazonaws.com
```

Example

```
aws ecr get-login-password --region ap-south-1 | docker login --username AWS --password-stdin 231145718278.dkr.ecr.ap-south-1.amazonaws.com
```

- Create a Dockerfile as explained in the images chapter.
- Build your Docker image using the following command:

   Syntax

```
docker build -t image_name .
```

   Example

```
docker build -t ubuntu-http .
```

- After the build is complete, tag your image.

Syntax

```
docker tag image aws_account_id.dkr.ecr.region.amazonaws.com/repository
```

Example

```
docker tag ubuntu-http:latest 231145718278.dkr.ecr.ap-south-1.amazonaws.com/ubuntu-http:latest
```

- Run the following command to push this image to your newly created AWS repository:

Syntax
```
docker push image_name
```

Example
```
docker push 231145718278.dkr.ecr.ap-south-1.amazonaws.com/ubuntu-http:latest
```

You can verify the pushed image at amazon ECR repository

On-premises repository

The open-source Docker registry and distribution, as well as a commercially supported version known as Docker Trusted Registry, are options if you prefer to maintain an on-premises repository and do not want to use the public repository because of security or infrastructure constraints.

Chapter 14

Deploy our containerized app

In this chapter, we will see a practical example of the application with three containers: the first of MongoDB, the second of the of the http server, and the third of MongoDB Express for managing MongoDB.

Create a MongoDB container.

First, we will create a Docker network.
```
docker network create db-network
```

Our application and MongoDB will communicate via this network.

```
$ docker network ls
NETWORK ID      NAME          DRIVER    SCOPE
c7ebebd14c23    bridge        bridge    local
387ae8ea1790    db-network    bridge    local
89fb0632c109    host          host      local
3b70dc57ea0d    none          null      local
```

Create a mongoDB container
```
docker run -d --network db-network --name mongodb \
-p 27017:27017 \
-e MONGO_INITDB_ROOT_USERNAME=admin \
-e MONGO_INITDB_ROOT_PASSWORD=password \
mongo
```

Create a Mongo Express container for Mongo database administration.

```
docker run -d --network db-network --name mongo-express \
-p 8081:8081 \
-e ME_CONFIG_MONGODB_SERVER=mongodb \
-e ME_CONFIG_MONGODB_ADMINUSERNAME=admin \
-e ME_CONFIG_MONGODB_ADMINPASSWORD=password \
-e MONGO_INITDB_ROOT_PASSWORD=password \
mongo-express
```

Because Mongo Express exposes the 8081 port, you may test the connection by visiting http://localhost:8081 in the server GUI or entering the server IP and 8081 port on another PC.

If prompted for a password, the default username is admin and the password is pass.

If it opens you up to this stage, you can be confident that the communication between MongoDB and the Mongo Express container is working properly.

Now, we'll generate the third image containing our app.
First, write a Dockerfile for the application in your application directory.

```
FROM node
RUN mkdir  /app/ && chown -R node:node /app
WORKDIR /app
COPY . /app
USER node
RUN npm install
COPY --chown=node:node . .
EXPOSE 8080
CMD [ "node", "server.js" ]
```

Once the image is complete, push it to the public repository so that it may be shared with other systems.
To orchestrate all three images, we construct the compose file, which launches the entire application stack.

Create a file called myapp.yaml or compose.yml like that.

```
version: '3'
services:
  mongodb:
    image: skgoyal1/app1:mongo
    ports:
      - 27017:27017
  mongo-express:
    image: skgoyal1/app1:mongo-express
    ports:
      - 8081:8081
  nodejs:
```

```
image: skgoyal1/app1:nodejs
ports:
  - 3000:3000
```

Once all containers are up and running, you can test your application. This is just one modest example of a container in operation; in real life, the applications are more complex.

www.ingramcontent.com/pod-product-compliance
Lightning Source LLC
Chambersburg PA
CBHW050234230526
45470CB00005B/1948